ORANGERY OF DREAMS

AND OTHER STORIES

A Collection of Short Stories by

TK SEEHRA

TK SEEHRA

All the characters in this book are fictitious, and any resemblance to actual persons, living or dead, is purely coincidental.

Copyright © TK Seehra 2015

All rights reserved

ISBN-13: 978-1517705688

DEDICATION

I dedicate Orangery of Dreams and Other Stories to my parents Mr & Mrs S Bansel. Without your encouragement, I would never have taken this journey into the written word world. Your support, faith in me and unconditional love has always given me hope and encouragement to follow my heart and pursue my dreams.

Thank you for everything.

TK SEEHRA

Orangery of Dreams and Other Stories is part 1 of a collection of short stories in the series, *A Splash of Colour.*

Part 2, *The Fault in Chillies and Jam and Other Stories* and Part 3, *Colour around You and Other Stories* are due to release soon.

CONTENTS

	Acknowledgements	Pg 1
1	Orangery of Dreams	Pg 2
2	Crying Crimson	Pg 13
3	Buffalo Wings	Pg 23
4	Tantalising Tea	Pg 32
5	Kindled Kindness	Pg 39
6	Tut Tut…Bang Bang	Pg 47
7	All A Bit Silly And All A Bit Right	Pg 54

TK SEEHRA

ACKNOWLEDGEMENTS

I wish to personally thank the following people for their help and support to me in creating this book:

My Husband- Thank you for being my sounding board every time I wrote a short story. You listened with patience and love. You were listening, right?!

My Kids- Thank you to my young daughters for bringing so much joy to my world and for letting me have time to write, even if that usually meant, me working whilst you both napped!

Amrit Bansel- Thank you for printing all my drafts for me. Your help enabled me to start the reviewing process.

Rita Chakraborty and Sophie Pathan- Thank you for your time proofreading and editing my work. Your input has been invaluable.

Arvinder Sambei- Thank you for your honesty and your input.

My family, friends and well-wishers- Thank you to everyone who has encouraged me along the way and offered their support and encouragement.

And finally, sending huge over pouring bucket loads of gratitude to God for always being my guiding light. Thank You for everything.

Front cover illustration ©ollinka2 / Fotolia

1 ORANGERY OF DREAMS

You know that feeling you get when you think you've lost your most precious item of jewellery or you've just broken your most treasured possession? You know that feeling of being frozen with the thought of impending doom and that notion that you've just done something so stupid that you just can't change it or reverse time? Well, that was how Mr. Londia felt when he realised he had left his winning lottery ticket on the bus.

He had been making big plans since he had discovered his win. He had been planning a party, travel, a change of house, a new car and a fountain of gifts for Mrs. Londia. Mrs. Londia had been busy planning too. She was ready to give half away to their children, a quarter away to her favourite charity and was planning on splitting that last quarter in two and saving half and enjoying the other half by buying little luxuries and paying for a summer orangery.

The orangery had always been a dream project of hers and although, with that kind of win, they could have afforded a huge house with an orangery included, she wanted to keep the house they lived in and just make changes to update and modernise it. The real indulgence for her was her orangery, which she had grand plans for entertaining in.

Zara loved entertaining and having people over. It gave her a chance to put her hair in an elegant up-do and a chance to wear those pretty frocks she had bought when she used to accompany Sathi to all those company dinners. It gave her an opportunity to wear her beautiful pearl earrings and her soft-as-air shawls. Somehow, in her head, having an orangery translated into having an ideal place for her to whip out her heels too.

When Sathi told Zara about the win, she felt like her heart was dancing. It was such good news and after all those years of putting money into the lottery, it felt like they deserved the win, or even were owed it.

When Sathi found out about the win, his heart nearly stopped. He felt a strange sense of fright at all that money as well as a sense of euphoria. How would he hide it all?

Would he tell everyone? Would he finally pack in the thankless job he had given so many years of his life to? Would he stick with it for his colleagues and for his sanity in order to stay normal now that he had so much money to his name?

There were so many questions and so many possibilities. Life seemed full of colour, optimism and wonder. There were choices; there were hopes, dreams and ideas. There were stories waiting to be told of adventure, surprise and gratitude. It was all so overwhelming and yet so perfect.

Now that he had returned home and his pockets had been checked for the 35th time, the realisation of what had been, could have been and what was now to be was debilitating. How could it have all come to this? There was embarrassment, shame, crippling anxiety and a strange stress that played on his mind. He felt jumpy, judged and justifiably jittery. How would he tell Mrs. Londia of the misfortune that had befallen them? How would he even bring himself to utter those words? How would he live knowing the orangery she had wanted for all those years had been in reach moments before and now seemed so far away again? Worse was knowing that it seemed so far away again entirely because of his own stupidity.

He had taken the lottery ticket out of his pocket for the 33rd time that day but only the third time on that bus. He felt he had to keep checking it to first just check he had the ticket, second to check the numbers again and third just so he could feel happy that he had won such a huge amount. It was on that 33rd time that he monetarily got distracted by an argument that broke out in the seat behind him.

The young girl told the young boy she was sitting next to that she had had enough and they had to go their separate ways. His friends behind him pretended not to be eavesdropping either but, just like Mr. Sathi Londia, they just couldn't help but be drawn into that world of 'it's all too late'.

With his ego bruised, the young boy started raising his voice and spluttering hateful words of poison. The young girl even got up once and tried to move past him but he pulled her arm and put his legs on the back of the seat in front of them making a barrier. She asked him to move, politely and then harshly, but he refused to move, telling her to sit back down.

On the other side where Mr. Londia sat, an old man turned on hearing the commotion and asked her if she was OK and if she wanted any help. She clearly needed help but she said she was OK, forcing him to turn back around and mind his own business. Some more commotion followed and then finally the young boy got up and said to her, 'You talk to me like that? You talking to *me* like that? You got some nerve you have. Your greasy hair, your big round glasses, your ugly-as-hell clothes. Don't know what I saw in you, you ugly piece of shit!' He was shaking his body, full of rude boy attitude before adding the final blow: 'Am gonna fuck Ria proper tonight. Am gonna show her what a real man can do. And you know what, she'll be smiling! Sore but smiling. Not miserable like you.'

Mr. Londia was disgusted. Was this how the youth of today talked? Was this the level of respect they gave one another? As he watched the boy get off the bus he pondered how young he actually was. Surely he was too young for a relationship? Surely he didn't mean that thing he said about Ria?

He turned to look at the girl who sat there looking like her world had just fallen apart. He had to do something, he had to say something. As he got up to join her, the man who had been sitting on the other side of Mr. Londia had already gotten up and was sitting next to the young girl and trying to console her.

Mr. Londia smiled and then just made his way to the bottom of the bus. His stop came and he was off. Moments later, his heart nearly stopped when he realised he had left the ticket. Surely it wasn't true? Surely he couldn't have been so distracted to have left the ticket on the bus. He checked his pocket for the 34th time that day with that heavy feeling of knowing he wouldn't find what he had wanted.

He went home that day as if a dark cloud was hovering above his head threatening thunderstorms and hailstones. His footsteps felt heavy and his body was slumped. So down and so totally brow-beaten, he felt his world crash around him. He saw visions of his wife crying and telling him he was a fool. He saw visions of her crying and putting her head down in shame at having such a foolish, absent-minded husband. He could even hear her curse her kismet and tell her sisters what an idiot he was.

When he got into the house he wanted to cry. Grown men didn't cry so his normal response was anger. Why didn't *she* take the ticket? Yes, he was angry at *her*. She should have looked after it; she should have taken the responsibility. It was all her fault. It was, wasn't it?

His anger at her was short-lived when he saw her through the kitchen window in the garden tending to the vegetables growing in their mini greenhouse. How could he be angry at her? How could he be angry at the lady who was watering his courgettes and pumpkins? How could he be angry at her, the one who loved him and had always made do in their humble home?

She turned and saw him through the window and waved at him. She smiled knowing their fortunes were changing; he nervously smiled knowing it was all over. How would he tell her? How would he break the news? How would they recover from this?

He went straight to his study/library/spare room and looked around him. This was it. It was here he was going to live and die alone in. It was here that Mrs. Londia would mock him for his stupidity. But what if she was OK with it all? What if she showered him with love and told him not to worry? What if she said the money didn't matter to her and she was the happiest woman alive just to be Mrs. Londia? What if she said she didn't care for the orangery, the money or any of it and was happy with what they collectively brought into the house?

Who was he kidding? He was distraught and knew she would be too.

When she came from the garden she called out to him. Where was he? Why wasn't he at the kitchen table with a cup of tea in one hand and the newspaper in the other? After checking the bedroom she went to the study/library/spare room and saw him staring at the ceiling. When she called out to him, he panicked and darted up and then did something very strange. He went to hide behind the table and sat curled up in a ball.

'What are you doing?' asked Zara, puzzled, and after hearing no response she asked again and went over to him. Frightened and scared, he looked at her as if she was going to eat him alive or rip his skin off and feed it to a group of ravenous bears. He looked at her and spluttered,

'I've done something terrible. I don't know what to do. It was a mistake, an accident. I don't know how it happened. I don't know what to do. I feel like I'm going to explode. I feel like it's all over! It is over. It's all finished…everything.' He looked at her confused face and added, 'I'm sorry. I don't know what else to say. I'm just so sorry.'

Stern-faced, Zara asked him, 'What's happened?'

He looked at her and felt daggers piercing his eyes and tornadoes sweeping up the room's contents and lodging them in his mouth, hindering his ability to talk.

'What's happened?' she repeated. 'Tell me? You look like you've committed a crime,' she said and then seeing his face drop, she added, 'What have you done? What's happened? You're frightening me now. Tell me what's happened?'

When he told her about the ticket she cursed her good-for-nothing husband. How could she console him when she was so angry and so distraught? They had come so close to having everything they ever wanted in monetary terms and now they were just where they were days before. Now they were back to a place where an orangery was only a dream again and not a real, possible, actuality.

The truth was that although they were back there in that place before the ticket, so much had changed. They were frustrated and unhappy, anxious and sad. They argued, they fought and they brought up their misfortune in regular conversations. She felt hard done by and he felt an idiot. It was all such a waste of energy on something that once could have been.

Mr. Londia cursed that damn lottery ticket. Had they not had it and not won and lost the ticket, they would have been OK and happy where they were. They had been too quick to weave such big dreams. They had been too quick to forget that there was life before that ticket and that that life was OK.

It was probably a good four or five years later that the arguments and the comments of their misfortune finally started to fade away. Mr. Londia forgave himself over the years as he finally accepted that the money was just never meant to be theirs. Maybe they really had everything they needed and maybe the money would have just added problems and complexity to their lives that they just did not need.

Mrs. Londia finally forgave her husband for losing that ticket too. Maybe splitting the money as she had thought would probably have caused more problems. Maybe she was just meant to make do with what she already had.

Sitting on the swing bench in their garden, with her husband next to her, Zara said, 'It's a double rollover this week. Shall we try our luck?'

Mr. Londia looked at her and smiled. 'A double rollover? How much could we win?'

'Twenty million pounds.'

'Twenty million pounds…that's a nice sum!'

'I thought so. Twenty million pounds…I could buy myself a few things with that,' she said with excited eyes.

'I think you could buy a bit more than a few things!'

'Maybe! I might actually get my orangery after all!' she said laughing.

'Let's hope so.' said Mr. Londia thinking about how far they had come. Sitting next to him was his wife, full of hope, passion and excitement. That lost ticket seemed like a distant and vague memory as the possibility of a new ticket and new hope promised the chance of abundance and joy. 'Fine, let's do it, let's try our luck…on one condition though.'

'Name it.'

'You keep the damn ticket this time!'

'Done,' she said smiling. 'And if we win, I'm getting my orangery.'

'Done,' he said smiling.

2 CRYING CRIMSON

'It's Ravi. There, I've said it. He's cheating on me,' she finally said to Aliya.

'He's what?'

'He's cheating on me,' Manji said casually before adding the crushing finality to the situation. 'It's over, me and him are finished.'

Aliya didn't know what to say. How had it all come to this? Manji and Ravi were perfect for one another. They were a star couple. He had done everything for her so how could he cheat on her? He had been everyone and everything for her so how could he do it? He had been her world and she had been his, so how did it all get to this?

After the shock, Aliya was angry; angry with Ravi and with Manji too. Where was Manji's anger? Where was her emotion? Where were her tears?

Manji had suspected Ravi for a while. The signs had been there for a while but she just didn't stop to read them. She ought to have questioned him long before but she didn't. She ought to have confronted him long before but she didn't. She just passed time and as her suspicions grew and festered, he carried on oblivious to her mind's activity.

She saw him sneaking out of the house when he thought she was sleeping, she saw him take phone calls out in the garden and she even caught him taking out of a tin an exquisite necklace that from a distance looked like diamonds and crimson gems. Maybe she could have overlooked it all, although the necklace did grate her, had it not been for the day she saw him sitting with another woman having coffee.

The other woman sat in a crimson-coloured dress…just the way Manji would have imagined an evil temptress to dress. She had flawless skin and elegance about her…just the type that made Manji feel sick. She giggled away at Ravi's jokes, just the way Manji had done years before. She smelt the flowers Manji had seen him give her, just the way Manji had done years before.

Her groomed hair and painted nails felt like insults to Manji who barely had time to brush her hair in the morning. Her sleek bag sat beside her reminding Manji of her oh so practical big, boring and functional bag. Her elegant pearl studs and pearl bracelet were the vision of class as Manji grimaced at the thought of forgetting to put any jewellery on at all that day.

Instead of confronting him that night she withdrew and dwelled on comparing herself to her. She sat making inane lists in her head of how she fell short of being Ravi's perfect woman. How had it all come to this? Had she caused this? Maybe if she had spent more time looking after herself he wouldn't have looked elsewhere. Maybe if she paid him more attention, he would not have been bewitched by the Devil. Maybe if she had worn a crimson dress, he would never have left her side.

It was of course useless thinking like that. The damage had been done and she knew it. When those thoughts subsided, the tears fell. They crashed, smashed and obliterated everything. Her eyes were swollen and her heart and ego bruised. Was this what happened after all those years of togetherness?

After the tears, came anger. Raw and painful anger.

Crimson anger. Spluttering and defenseless anger. How could he? How could he be so heartless? How could he after all those years together jeopardise it? How could he do it after all those vows? How and why?

When the confrontation happened, he didn't see her anger coming. He had been tip-toeing around her for so long now that he had thought she would remain oblivious. He had tried to cover his tracks but some clues just slipped out giving his game away. He had even hidden all the evidence but Manji had gotten wind of it.

Her face contorted and expletives exploded everywhere. Accusations were hurled and fists thumped. Eyes watered and tempers flared. Voices were raised and pride was dented. It was all so ugly, all so messy.

He couldn't deny it. He had been taking secret calls from someone and yes he had bought jewellery. When she spoke of the woman in the crimson dress he was unable to deny that he had sat there and was making her laugh. How could he deny any of it? How could he concoct a story that saved him? How could he concoct a story that would appease her?

'Sorry,' he said as he got up and went over to hug her. His hug was vehemently refused.

Her eyes crimson with rage, she said, 'Sorry! Is that all

you've got to say?'

He looked at her pitiable state and walked away as he heard her blurt, 'Go to hell you cheating bastard.'

He wanted to say something to calm her down, he wanted to give her a hug and he wanted a chance to explain. But there was too much hurt and too much upset.

Manji cried a crimson ocean that day. Her Ravi had cheated on her and all he had said was sorry. Maybe it was better that way. Maybe hearing details or explanations would have been too much for her. Maybe hearing about when it all started or how long it had been going on for would be enough to tip her over the edge. Maybe this is why she had had two miscarriages. Maybe she wasn't meant to be a mum because this day would have made it all the uglier.

The day was ugly and all of a sudden her grief gave way to her feeling ugly. How had ugliness crept up on her? How had ugliness led him to her? How had ugliness immobilised her sense of worth? Ugliness was everywhere and in everything. It sat in her pots and pans and hid under the stairs. It jumped on their bed and swam in the sink. Everything was splashed with ugliness apart from that necklace she remembered full of diamonds and crimson gems. That was beautiful.

That night she locked Ravi out of their bedroom and Ravi found himself sleeping on the sofa. A part of her wanted him to knock down the door and say it had all been untrue or a huge misunderstanding. A part of her wanted to hear him plead for her to open the door and a part of her wanted him to cry a crimson ocean too. But he didn't do anything. He just took out a spare duvet from the cupboard and brought out the biscuit tin to munch on as they had done on many a movie night.

The next day she came out of the room and he was nowhere to be seen. It was then she realised that it was over. It was then she realised that they were never meant to make 10 years together.

Aliya had left their house that day in disbelief. Her two best friends were breaking up and when Manji had told her that Ravi had been cheating on her, she felt sickened. She knew how much he loved Manji and wanted to know how he could do this to her after all those years together. Instead of going straight home she found her legs taking her straight to Ravi's accountancy firm.

She knew it wasn't her place to get angry and confront him but what else could she do? Manji's quiet acceptance irritated her. She had seen them go through so much that to call it quits after so long just didn't make sense.

Ravi took one look at Aliya and laughed. He knew why she was here. He knew that despite her being his friend first, right now she stood united with his wife. He also knew she too believed it all.

'Liya, Manji's spoken to you, right'? Aliya nodded.

'She's told me everything.'

'She has, has she?' Seeing her nod, he added, 'Why don't we sit and have a coffee. I'll explain.' Aliya nodded.

'Fine.'

Ravi looked at one of his colleagues on the adjacent desk and said, 'Half hour if the boss asks.'

He told Aliya everything over coffee and at her insistence agreed to speak to Manji that evening.

Manji was ready to leave the house for time out when he got back. He stopped her and said they needed to talk.

'Liya met me,' he said, looking at those sullen eyes.

'She met me too,' she mumbled.

'She wanted me to speak to you. Manji, look at me.'

Slowly she gazed up at him as she wondered if he had tempted the other woman or if she had tempted him.

'Manji, what's got into you?'

'Me? What's got into me? What's got into *you*? How could you do this to *me*? How could you do this to *us*? How could you...'

'That's enough. I would have told you yesterday but you shut me out.'

'I should have done more than that! I should have...'

He had to tell her about everything. He had to break the news to her. All that secrecy had backfired. He hadn't been cheating on her. All the secrecy had been for a surprise 10th wedding anniversary party he had been planning.

'But who was that lady in the red dress?' she asked, not quite believing him.

'She was doing the flowers for the tables.'

'I saw you giving her flowers.'

'You certainly did. They were the flowers I wanted her to arrange for the centerpiece.'

'And what about the necklace I saw you hold?'

His face dropped. She had seen that too.

'You didn't see the tin box it came out of?'

She shook her head. He went to get the box and the necklace. 'It's yours! It was going to be a surprise but here you go! I'd rather we made it to ten years! It's yours.'

She held the tin box which encased the necklace full of diamonds and crimson gems and opened it to unveil its magnificence.

'Tin and diamonds, Manji, the symbols of being married for ten years. Look, I even got it engraved for you,' he said as he showed her the side of the tin box. 'To my beautiful Manji, my life, my wife, my world. Happy 10th Wedding Anniversary. With all my love forever, your Ravi.' Ravi looked at his wife's sullen face and then added, 'Believe me now?'

There was no place for doubt; the engraving had confirmed it all. Manji felt a deeply embarrassed fool. Why had she doubted him? Why hadn't she looked for another explanation to it all? Why had she hurt Ravi and herself by thinking and hurling such hateful accusations?

Manji nodded, 'I believe you.' After a moment's pause, she added, 'Sorry…for everything. I should have trusted you, I should have…I'm a terrible wife, aren't I?'

'Hmm, you're OK I guess!' he said as he looked her in the eyes. 'I should be angry with you. You made me sleep on the sofa! I finished all the biscuits in the tin and probably put on a stone thanks to you!'

'Sorry!'

'But, you know, I'm not angry, Manji. I know you did it because you love me. I know you did it because you caught me being a bit secretive. I just wanted to surprise you. I just wanted to see my Manji's face when everyone shouted "surprise" and I gifted you this necklace. So I'm sorry for wanting to surprise my wife!'

'And I'm sorry I didn't let you surprise me!' Looking at the necklace full of diamonds and crimson gems, she added, 'This is beautiful, so beautiful. Thank you.'

When Ravi had told Aliya about the surprise that day, Aliya had laughed and insisted he told Manji the truth before matters got out of hand. Luckily he did and after the embarrassment and the apologies, Manji and Ravi joined together to finalise plans for their wedding anniversary party, which although no longer a surprise, was the perfect opportunity to paint the town crimson.

3 BUFFALO WINGS

'That's enough butter and chilli don't you think?' she said in that tone that always felt so condescending to him. He wanted to retort back and tell her to take over but he kept quiet. He always kept quiet when she entered the kitchen. He knew that to say anything was to invite trouble. There was too much at stake today and too much to get right. His family were coming to see them and he wanted everything to be perfect. He wanted everything looking pristine, everything cooked to perfection and he wanted everything to go his way.

As they entered the driveway she said, 'Right on time,' and then as if on cue he looked at her and before he had a chance to lovingly gaze at her beautiful frame and beautiful ringlets, she added the blow: 'Just an hour and half late!' He sighed. His face dropped and then he shook himself together and opened the door. There they were, in his driveway, and getting ready to walk down that beautifully cobbled path that he and his brother had painstakingly laid down some 15 years ago. It was a labour of love that warmed his brother's heart every time he came down to visit.

His brother remembered the two of them laying those cobbled stones into the cement, trying to make a pattern. He remembered how their father looked at them from inside the house, observing their work whilst sipping away at his tea. He remembered how their father would come out every now and again and warm their hearts with stories of the past and dreams of the future. Every time he visited his brother Saini, it all came flooding back.

'So nice to see you,' Saini said to his brother Jaan and his wife as he opened his arms ready to hug those adorable children of theirs. With smiles on their faces, they ran into his arms.

'Uncle, we made it.'

He smiled, 'That I can see...so you made it past the lions and the tigers?'

'Oh just about! It was a close one though! You see, today the lions and the cheetahs were let loose,' said Lalaya.

'Really? You'll have to tell me all about it!' he said as he looked excitedly at his wife who never seemed to share his enthusiasm at the animal stories that always came when they visited.

Lyla had heard so many stories over the years and each

time, when Saini humored them, she always felt a tinge of agitation and distress. So many animals, so many stories came out of that imaginative little mind that she often wondered if Lalaya would ever shut up.

Maybe it was because they did not have children themselves that she was always so irked by them. Maybe it was because they were not blessed with angels that she always saw mischievous evil in them. Maybe it was because they did not have toys in their house, that their house was always so clean. Maybe it was nothing to do with them not having children, and maybe it was just that she found *these* children so irritating.

She tried to hide her disgust when Manaya, the eldest child, accidently knocked over one of the empty tea cups on the floor. Manaya looked up at Lyla and innocently apologised, just like her mother had always taught her to if an accident occurs. It was lucky enough that there was no tea left in the cup but had that bone china tea cup broken, Saini would have heard it, on repeat, like a broken record, over and over again into the early hours of the night. She never understood why he always got the bone china tea set out for their visit knowing fully well that they always would bring Manaya and Lalaya with them.

Entering the kitchen with the empty cups, she saw him finishing of his creation. It looked like a work of art or certainly something that she would be proud to showcase during one of her countless evenings of entertaining and

25

perfect for cocktail hour. Why did he never make that much effort with her friends or her family?

'What do you think?' he said as he showed her his work.

'Nice,' and then unable to hold herself back, she added, 'It's a lot of food, a hell of a lot of food! This is probably a week's worth of food, or enough food to feed an army.'

'Honey,' he whispered. 'Shh, they'll hear us. Look, if the army inside doesn't eat it, we'll have it tomorrow. You know what that means?' he said as he paused for a bit and then added, 'No cooking! Now come on, they're waiting inside.'

Saini left the kitchen and walked back into the sitting room with an impressive array of hors d'oeuvres displayed on a beautiful, round, acacia platter. He had done it again! He had somehow managed to delight the senses by uniting world flavours altogether in harmony. She would never have thought of mixing so many different foods together on one plate but somehow Saini's creation just seemed to work. There was Italian bruschetta, Indian paneer with chutney, Spanish tapas, Mexican taquitos, Greek tzatziki and Moroccan humus all neatly presented and looking so inviting on that platter.

Before his impressed guests had a chance to get stuck in, he whizzed back to the kitchen and brought out another round platter. This time, he had calamari soaked in orange, mozzarella coated in thyme, caviar on bread, a selection of fine cheeses, cured meats along with some humble carrot and celery sticks that sat sheepishly beside his signature appetiser.

'Enjoy!' he said and just before he sat down he remembered what he had prepared for the kids. Saini looked at Lyla and said, 'Honey, grab me the kids' platter.' His brother looked at him with a look of amazement; how thoughtful of him to have thought of the kids as well.

Dutifully Lyla went to the kitchen and returned with the kid's platter that delighted their eyes. Chips, nuggets, sandwiches and mini pizzas would always win over such adult delicacies. It was at times like this that Manaya and Lalaya would be won over again and again. It was at times like this that they reasserted between themselves that Uncle Saini was indeed their favourite uncle.

Uncle Indy, their father's cousin brother, came a close second, but he always spent so much time in front of the TV and was always so busy with their Dad that he never seemed to have any real time for them. He was a close second because whenever Manaya and Lalaya would visit he would always, at the end of their visit, have gifts waiting for them. Somehow, he always knew what to get them and despite how bored they were during their visit, all was always forgotten when their eyes beamed with joy at their new gifts.

'Saini,' his brother said later that evening. 'You did amazing, really amazing. I'm so stuffed!'

'Good, you really think I did amazing?'

'No question, the food was out of this world, you really know your stuff!'

Saini looked at him and smiled and modestly said, 'I tried; I wasn't sure how the calamari would come out. Think I might not have used enough orange...'

'Saini, it was the business! And those buffalo wings, well, they took me right back to our childhood. Right back to those days when mum would make them...you got the butter and chilli spot on!'

'Really?' Saini asked as if for more approval.

'Oh yeah, it was just lovely! You know, I'll be hearing it for days now,' he said as he got ready to mimic his wife, clearing his throat. 'You call this food! You call this piece of bread food! You need to go and stay with Saini and learn how to cook. If he can do it for Lyla, why can't you do it for me! Call yourself an,' he paused and looked at Saini and in unison they both laughed and said, 'American Indian!' Both of them sighed, shook their heads and burst out into school-boy laughter.

In an instant they were transported back home, back to those days when life seemed simpler and love was pure. There they were in the warmth of their childhood home where frames adorned the walls and photos captured their achievements. There they were in a place where love oozed from every corner and crevice in their home. There they were in a place where the smell of warm bread used to greet them in the morning and music would cascade in their house, breaking up the tranquil calm. There they were playing together in the snow, drawing with crayons on the walls and then protecting each other when they were caught red-handed.

Later that evening, Lyla noticed a smirking Saini and said, 'What's happened?'

He looked at his wife in that beautiful black laced gown and smiled. How did she do that? How did she always seem to know when he was happy or sad? How did she always seem to know something else was going on when it was? Why was he so useless at hiding his thoughts from her?

'Everything,' he said as if by saying everything, everything would make sense to her.

'What do you mean?' she questioned as she snuggled up to him.

'It's all ours!' he said, hardly containing his joy. 'Everything...every last drop!'

'What?' she said, darting off him. 'What do you mean everything?'

And as he explained, her heart dropped. How could Saini have done it? How could her husband take what was never meant to be his or hers? She felt as if cayenne pepper had been sprayed into her eyes and thick, fatty butter had got stuck in her throat. Why had Saini done it? Why had he taken advantage of Jaan and after all that food got him to transfer their parents' inheritance to him?

'But I don't understand. Why, would you do it? Why today? Why after everything?' she asked him.

'Lyla, he didn't deserve it. It was never really his anyway. How he ended up with it in the first place is a mystery. He's a sweet talker; he must have sweet talked them into it. They always had a soft spot for him, even though it was me who did everything. It was me who helped them with everything. He never did anything. He never called; he hardly visited, he ...'

'Stop!' she cried. 'You should hear yourself! It was never yours! It was never meant to be yours! If it was meant to be yours, it would have been yours; they would have left it for you. It was theirs; his, hers, Lalaya's and Manaya's. It wasn't ours! It wasn't! I can't believe you...how could you? How could you? What haven't we got here? We've got everything...everything, more than we need.'

'I know, but honey, now we've got more!' he said as his eyes lighted up. 'And Jaan's a man of his word you know. I've just checked...all the money is in the account! Every last drop, it's all ours!'

Lyla felt suffocated. 'But why today? Why?'

'It had to be today! Today was the day Jaan would have given me the earth if I asked for it.'

'What?' she said looking at him in disbelief.

'Do you know what day it is today?'

'No!'

'Today's the day mum and dad adopted him 35 years ago…35 years ago! It's on this day, every year, that he uses his heart not his head. It's on this day, every year, that he's putty in my hands! I could get him to do anything…anything! And you know what sealed it today? Do you know what sealed it…it was those damn buffalo wings! All that time I spent cooking everything and making sure everything was perfect, and it was those damn buffalo wings that did it. Emotional fool!'

4 TANTALISING TEA

It was the smell of cardamom and fennel seeds in the air that made her feel sick in the throat. That smell, so sweet in years gone by, revolted her now. It grated her skin and felt like insects that had somehow crept in and were walking under her skin. How had she ever loved the taste?

It was Ansu who had made her her first cup of Indian tea. He laughed and mocked her for having spent all her life avoiding the stuff and having coffee instead. How had an Indian survived all those tea parties and all those years of not bringing saucepans to boil? It was quite unheard of and it made Ansu laugh.

Heera had sat with Ansu weaving dreams of tomorrow as she sipped on that first concoction which for many years would happily take the place of her normal beverage. It tantalised her senses and became a welcome addiction.

She had held his hand and heart and he had held hers.
The conversation flowed and was enjoyable. Time not
only passed; it skipped and did a merry dance.

That day they had talked about their fears and their
dreams. They had opened their hearts and souls and
connected with each other so much that they felt a kinship.
Could one really fall in love at first sight and in that very
first meeting? Heera wasn't sure but Ansu knew.

Ansu was right, love could happen and it did happen.
They enjoyed love's caress and got married the same year
in a small but intimate ceremony. They were friends,
lovers and in time became parents to four adorable
children.

Time passed and now here they were at this funny juncture
in life and it was as if someone had just pulled the sink
plug out of their lives and put the darkness into their day.
Why did it all seem so bleak? Why did the days seem so
unforgiving? Where had all the hope of a bright tomorrow
gone?

It had crept up on them and screamed 'Boo' from behind
their curtains. It had mingled in with their routines and
oddities. It had smothered them both in the day and in the
night. Heera had never thought that the passing of time

could be so cruel. Heera had never thought after all those years she would be sitting alone like this.

Heera had given her life to her family and Ansu had given his to his work. They had always talked about what they would do when they got to 40 and when that age passed, the goal post changed to 50, 60 and then 70. It was silly really; they ought to have done things along the way. They ought to have enjoyed their journey and reached their goals. They ought to have done so much by now.

Heera had turned 70 two weeks ago, ahead of Ansu by two and a half months. Where was the life they had pictured? When did time pass them by? There was so much to be done still but was there any time left? Was there still any time for them to live out their dreams?

Their children had all taken their paths and gone in the directions their hearts chose. They were left alone wondering why they had dedicated their lives to everyone but themselves. Rajan, their third child, had always encouraged them to travel and do things they wanted to. But now they wondered if it had all been left too late.

Heera had wanted to travel the world but somehow life just happened and her dreams of travel just never materialised. Somehow, with Rajan's help, she convinced

Ansu to start that epic journey across the world. Had they done it earlier they wouldn't have left with the extra baggage of arthritis and blood pressure, but as they hadn't, they had to take them with them.

The three other brothers tried to convince them not to go. It was too dangerous, too much, too everything...and the elephant in the room stomped and cackled too, too late. Surely now was the time that they should be taking things easy. Surely now was the time that they should be sitting indoors in the safety and comfort of their own home. What if they fell ill, what if they got hurt, what if something worse happened? Heera and Ansu heard everything and knew there were risks. But the risks of not doing anything and staying in the same place far outweighed the benefits of staying there. It was something they should have done years ago but they hadn't. It was something they needed to do now.

And so Heera and Ansu, much to the surprise of their three other sons, left the comforts of the home that they had lived in for years for a taste of travel and what really else was out there in the world.

They started off in Thailand and made their way through Malaysia. The amazing tastes rejuvenated their senses and reawakened their passion. This was the life they had dreamed of all those years back. Yes, this was where the magic was.

After a trip to Indonesia, they made their way to India. It was here that they felt a deep affinity with the culture and way of life. Living in their fast-paced lives, bringing up their children, working every hour God sent, they had forgotten the simple things. It was here that they decided to settle.

When they told their children that they would not be returning, their children thought they were crazy. They ought to do this and they ought to do that. But Ansu and Heera loved it out here. They felt free somehow of the shackles of life and pleasurably free. They were themselves and they were at peace. It felt lovely.

Manu, their second eldest son, a month into their stay urged them to come back and said that they had had enough time away. They were missing them and their grandchildren were missing them too. As much as it pulled on their heart strings, Heera said they were staying put. For the first time in years they were doing something for themselves and they wanted to embrace it as much as their hearts and souls allowed.

It was Ansu, who after three months away, said to his wife that it was time they returned. It was never meant to be a long stay and in fact the original plan had been to travel to a few spots around the world and return back in two months. Heera hated to admit it but as headstrong as she was, and as much as they had embraced this adventure, she was missing her children, her grandchildren and that old life. And so they decided to return.

Two and a half weeks into their return, Ansu passed away. It was a peaceful passing but a painful one all the same. Heera was beside herself with grief.

After the funeral, she refused to stay at any of her children's houses. She was still able and capable of looking after herself. She neither wanted to inconvenience anyone nor did she want to be inconvenienced. She just wanted to be.

In the comfort of her own room, she thought back to the happy memories she had had with Ansu and that three month adventure she had had with him. She was so glad to have lived some of her dreams with him and so glad that they had had time out together before he had left her.

It was five o'clock at the old people's home where Heera had now been for a couple of months and they were celebrating another year of India's independence. In honour of the day, along with snacks the chefs were brewing away a special concoction. It was a familiar smell that took Heera back to that first beverage that Ansu made for her.

When the catering staff came round with Indian tea and offered it to Heera she felt sickened and shook her head.

'Milk?'

She shook her head again and just like all those times before Ansu entered her life, she said, 'I'll have coffee.'

5 KINDLED KINDNESS

The morning dew glistened on the leaves and the roses smelt of perfume. The bluebells danced and the exotic Bird of Paradise flowers just looked stunning. The freshness of the rained-on herbs delighted and the beauty of the hedgerows charmed. The vegetable patch was full of promise and the pond was well looked after. It was in all that beauty and in all that freshness, that Devan sat counting his blessings.

He had been on an incredible journey and had paid an incredible price. He had longed for riches and longed for completeness. He had wanted a sense of finality and here he knew he had found it.

It had been a tumultuous ride and there had been times he had doubted he would ever get here. There had been times when he had wanted to call it a day. There had been times when it had all seemed so dark that his head hurt. There had been times when they had been so cruel that he had bitten his tongue. He had wanted to retaliate, he had wanted to fight and at times he had even wanted to cry. But he sat amidst all the madness and made friends with the dark side instead.

Grown men didn't cry, they got angry and went to hide in their caves. They didn't want to talk about it, they didn't want to relive it, they just wanted space. Space from everyone, space from everything and space from themselves.

The problem was when he got space, it suffocated him and scratched annoyingly deep inside his ears. His nose itched and his eyes felt tired and weary. He had been here so many times. He had felt this way so many times. He had laughed his way out after all that painful silence.

It had been seven years and he still struggled with it all. He had waited and waited but inspiration didn't come. He kept getting bulldozed by life's knocks and he just kept getting off target. He had tried desperately to recreate the magic but the magic just fizzled out and slipped through his fingers like grains of sand.

It was going to come. It was going to strike at any moment. He had told himself that for so many years that even she got tired. She got tired of waiting, she got tired of that same story and when it all got too much, Kirin left him.

Kirin had always encouraged him to achieve his goals. She had patiently rooted for him, privately prayed for him and publicly defended him. She knew there was more to him than the day job. She knew there was more he needed to achieve. She knew it would happen but she just didn't know when.

A part of her had always thought it would happen when she was with him. A part of her fantasised about being there in the crowd wearing a glamorous gown whilst he picked up an award and made his acceptance speech. A part of her fantasised that he would in his speech say how much of an inspiration and a muse she had been to him. He would be living the high life and so would she, just by being by his side.

It had always been the plan and he had always been determined to make it. When she had tired of waiting and grown tired of their relationship, they amicably went their separate ways. There was no bitter break up, there were no tears, no cheating, no cacophony of discord and certainly no desire on either of their parts to try and make it work. They were adults and they just grew apart. They were friends, but had stopped being lovers years ago. They were two people who at one time thought they were on the same path.

His path had always been the same. He wanted to write and he wanted to see his work in print. Her path had always been to be a doctor. After all those years in medical school, she became what she set out to become. For her it was a linear path and although his path was somewhat linear, it also had marked breaks, twists and turns.

He loved writing but when the words refused to flow he did other things. He trained as a mechanic, did a plumbing course, took up yoga, went travelling and even worked in an office job doing data entry. He dotted from this to that and jumped from here to there. He put his all into all he did but it was never really him. Kirin didn't understand it. If he wanted to write, why didn't he?

After she left he thought he'd be inspired to write again but he wasn't. It took a random act of kindness to propel him back to the world of words. He sat at *Sartaj's*, the local café, as he always did every Friday eating away at his English breakfast when he overheard a conversation from the table next to him.

The lady said to the man she was sitting with, 'Thank you.'

He looked at her and said, 'Anytime'. He picked up his coat and left the café and the lady burst out into tears. How could he make her cry?

Devan passed her a tissue and said,

'Would you like this?'

She looked at him, thanked him and took the tissue.

'Husband? Boyfriend? Friend upset you?' And then as if remembering himself he added, 'Sorry, that's really rude of me to ask.'

She looked up at Devan and said, 'It's OK. Truth is I don't know him. He just helped me out and it really touched me.' Devan looked at her and she added, 'My car broke down and he stopped to help. I was off to see my grandma in hospital and if it wasn't for him, I wouldn't have made it.'

'That's nice.'

'My grandma didn't make it; she passed away a few hours ago.'

'Oh, I'm sorry,' said Devan.

'It's OK, she was in pain. She'd suffered for far too long. But if I didn't make it in time to see her one last time, I'm not sure what I would have done. That guy made it happen and the only thank you he wanted was to see me smile. He joined me for a quick bite, which he didn't even let me pay for and now he's gone. I'll probably never see him again but I'm eternally grateful to him.'

'What a good soul.'

'An angel.'

That act of kindness stayed in Devan's mind the whole day. He kept thinking of that woman's tears, those few words she said to him and that man whom he had only heard saying 'Anytime'. Angels existed in this world and that man really was one of them. That night he serenaded serendipity as his angel muse visited him and Devan wrote to his heart's content. Words flowed and stories spilt out so freely that he felt liberated.

He wrote every day for the next four months and then it happened. A chain of events made him contact a publisher on Argyll Street and this time he actually got that call. Alexia Harris, deputy editor at Myla Publishers, agreed to print his work. His novel *Heartbeat* did really well and got his name known. After *Heartbeat*, the momentum was still there and he wrote *Mr. Kal's Kindness*, which was loosely based on that random conversation he had had with that lady in the café.

Mr. Kal's Kindness went on to be a bestseller and sold millions of copies worldwide. Devan became a well-known international bestseller and after all those years had the success he had only dreamed of.

Collecting the Man Booker prize was probably one of his finest moments. He thanked everyone who had inspired and encouraged him. He was humbled by his success and the recognition and dedicated his win to the random lady he had met in the café and that man who had helped her in her time of need.

In his beautifully landscaped garden he counted his blessings. He had had a phone call the day before from Kirin. Why did she call him after all those years? Did she want a part of the fame, the riches, and the recognition?

As their conversation unfolded it became clear. She wanted none of the fame, riches or recognition. She didn't even want to get back together with him as he half thought she might. She called to say thanks. Thanks for not losing hope and heart when she failed to encourage him and she thanked him for *Mr. Kal's Kindness.*

She said it made her feel grateful for all those people who had been a part of her life. It reminded her to be grateful for the knowledge she had, the work she did and the friends and family around her. She was sure she wouldn't have stopped to take time out and appreciate everything around her had she not read his book.

It was a lovely gesture to say thanks and that act of kindness made him smile. As he counted his blessings in the garden, he counted Kirin as one of his blessings too. She had taken time out to be kind just like the man in the café who had been kind to take out time to help that lady whose car had broken down. The lady who had broken down had been kind to take out time to see her grandma and had then been kind to take out time to say thank you to the man she called an angel. They were all like his character Mr. Kal, who had stopped for a moment in time to be kind.

All this kindness was wonderful. All this kindness was heartwarming and contagious. Devan smiled and gratefully thought, all this kindness made it all seem worthwhile.

6 TUT TUT…BANG BANG

It was underneath that tree that he sat with his father and said he was sorry. It had been so long since that time at the police station but they both remembered it like it was yesterday. They remembered details, like the clothes they were wearing, what they ate that day, who they had met and even that whole scene which would be forever etched in their minds.

Shanti, Roy's mum, had told them not to go out that day. There was something inauspicious in the air and her intuition forbade anyone from leaving the house. Her husband, Major Manas Rajan, and Roy paid little attention. They knew that if they paid attention to everything she said they would never get anything done, let alone leave the house.

At first Shanti's predictions used to be uncannily spot-on but with time and age they got a bit cloudy. She would talk about inviting the Devil's tongue and awaking the dead if you did this on a Monday or did that on a Thursday. For a town like Muzondo such tales were commonplace, but for the Shateriya family they were unusual and a sign of humour. What did she know? Such talk always sounded absurd and a little prehistoric.

Roy was the first and only child to Major Manas Rajan and Shanti. He was a spoilt brat and got everything he ever asked for. He had all the riches and all the comforts that the less-than-affluent families of Muzondo could only ever dream of. He was a handsome young man too and always managed to attract a bevy of beauties. Major Manas Rajan loved it but Shanti always felt a tad insecure, though she wouldn't admit it.

Shanti had always wanted him to settle with a nice Indian girl and hated that her son would be the one lad in the town who was probably on the top of the Most Not Ready to Settle Down for Marriage list, as he was always so busy romancing the girls in their town. Each and every girl felt special with him and thought they had a chance to sway him away from this life to a life where they were the centre of his universe.

It was only Monica who managed to come close to being

his centre of the universe. Monica was a softly spoken girl from the Jhalak family. She knew of his seductive ways and the more and more she tried to avoid his advances, the more and more she was drawn to him. When Shanti realised the grip Monica was having on her son she, behind closed doors, jumped on his bed twenty times and as if by magic Monica was never seen near their house again.

With Monica out of their lives, the Shateriya family returned to their normal ways again. Roy continued shooting birds and romancing women while Major Manas Rajan continued his work selling fire arms to those in Muzondo who needed them.

Shanti hated all the shooting but it brought in the money. She hated that her husband sold them and she hated that her son used them in sport. It was the venom of sixty-six snakes and the kiss of a mythical unicorn's curse. One day they would all have to pay for their association with them. She hoped that time would not come so soon but she knew it would come and in her life-time she would have to see it.

They paid for it on the holiest day in the Farika calendar. It was on the day of forgiveness and remembrance that it all happened. Roy's best friend Kalum took a firearm from Major Manas Rajan and threatened to kill a girl whom he had wanted to marry. The fair maiden had rejected his advances and the spurned and once valiant Kalum rode through Muzondo on his horse to open fire.

Blood was shed that day and the poor girl became another victim to the world. Kalum rode back and shared his tale of bravado with his chum Roy. They had no interest in joining in the street festivities but instead they indulged in talking, sharing stories and enjoying the heat from the fire that they were cooking a wild boar on.

Shanti hated the smell of wild boar cooking. It made her nails curls and her teeth feel smothered with soot. Early on she tried to discourage Roy from eating it but he enjoyed it too much. It was too late to influence him now. And so when that hideous smell made its way to her nose, she sighed. She knew Roy was with Kalum and she knew they were celebrating another evil.

When their stomachs were full they entered the Shateriya house and sprayed it with their grotesque laughter and their hideous conversation. Shanti avoided them but Roy called out to her and said, 'Another witch gone!'

Shanti looked at the pitiable two and shook her head. When were they ever going to make honest men of themselves?

'A big fat ugly witch!' added Kalum.

'Not good enough for our Kalum…tut tut…bang bang!' said Roy imitating a shooting.

'Tut tut…bang bang!' repeated Kalum. 'Just like that, just like that!'

Roy laughed as he saw his mother walk away.

'Who did she think she was, rejecting me? Rejecting me! Mr. Kalum Dhadladiya. Rich son of Mr. and Mrs. Dhadladiya of Garpur in Muzondo!'

'Who did she think she was?'

'Monica Jhalak…the witch!'

Roy froze and then said, 'Who?'

'What do you mean, who?'

'That name you just said?'

'Monica Jhalak?'

Roy's eyes turned to ice as his head burned in flames. Pulsating anger burst inside him as he calmly excused himself. Returning from his room, he hid a shotgun in his top. More blood was shed that night.

Shanti heard the gunshot and came running down the stairs. Seeing her son standing beside a dead Kalum, she howled. What had happened here? How had friends become enemies? How had her son gotten blood on his hands?

Roy offered no explanation and when Major Manas Rajan came home he understood everything. He told his son they were to leave the house immediately and they needed to arrange an alibi. As they left the house, Major Manas Rajan told Shanti not to move the body and that they wouldn't be long.

As they made their way to the town centre Major Manas Rajan told Roy to wait on the bench while he made some enquiries. Roy waited to see what his father would arrange and, moments later, two men came. They stood there with his father and then told Roy he was under arrest. He was under arrest for thieving a firearm from his dad's shop, for using it without a license, and for killing a man. Being in that police station was just the beginning of a long sentence he was due to receive.

It was many years later that Roy was released from prison and reunited with his parents. He was sorry for what he had done and under the tree, he apologised to his father. He did it because Kalum killed Monica. He did it because Monica disappeared from his life without explanation. He did it because she vanished out of his life the same week he was preparing to make an honest man of himself and propose to her.

When Shanti learned of the whys she thought back to the jumping on the bed. Without even realising it she had played a part in all this mess and to offer herself in forgiveness she took to the bed and cut her toe nails and placed them on her stomach and said a few words. It was later that day that Major Manas Rajan discovered his wife was no more.

7 ALL A BIT SILLY AND ALL A BIT RIGHT

'Help!' said Mr. Kericha as he sat looking up out of that hole. What a silly thing to have done to have fallen down in the first place. What a silly thing to have done whilst wearing odd socks and an ill-fitting top that showcased his midriff. What a silly thing to have done to have let the parrot out of her cage. It was all a bit silly and it was all a bit too late.

When Mr. Kericha fell down the hole he was lucky to have not broken his bones or bled to death. When he fell down he was lucky not to have soiled his underwear or to have further hurt his burnt arm.

He had burnt his arm earlier that day and it was stinging. He had been cooking and carelessly had placed a wet spoon into a hot wok of oil. The splattering of oil luckily missed his face but his arm got a few splutters. Still, he was lucky that it was only a few splutters and nothing too serious.

In preparation for Janki's visit later that day, he had been cooking up a stir-fry with bamboo shoots and water chestnuts. It was Janki's favourite food and Mr. Kericha had been hoping to impress her. But not only had he left the kitchen in a mess, he had burnt his arm and fallen down a hole. Janki was sure to be anything but impressed.

Janki had met Mr. Kericha through an on-line dating agency. He had described himself as an honest, lovable and hard-working individual who loved to cook, travel and take long walks. Janki loved long walks and so she took a gamble and got in contact.

That first meeting was a memorable one. Janki was expecting a tall, dark and handsome young man and instead got a short, pot-bellied man of average looks. He had expected a young, pretty girl with beautiful long hair and he had got it. When they saw each other they both stuttered; he at his good luck and her at her questionable luck. From a distance they seemed a bit ill-matched but in that first meeting they shared so much in common that they felt cheery and quite at ease.

Their first date was made all the more memorable because Mr. Kericha fell flat to the ground after tripping on a lady's handbag. It wasn't just any lady's handbag; it was Janki's favourite tan-coloured designer handbag. When he fell, everyone in the coffee shop stopped to stare. When he fell, everyone noticed the young-looking Janki leap up to try and help him back up. When he fell, all Janki noticed was that although he laughed at the fall, his eyes told of his embarrassment.

It wasn't just memorable because of Mr. Kericha's fall, it was also memorable because just as Janki went to sit down, her blouse button popped out and nearly took out Mr. Kericha's eye. She was so embarrassed she didn't know where to look. Her face went red and she could feel tears forming. How stupid of her to have left her pashmina at home. How silly of her to have left her cardigan and coat at home too.

Mr. Kericha looked at Janki and passed her his coat. How could she take a coat from a man she had just met? But then if she didn't, how would she get back home all exposed?

Graciously she accepted the coat and said she'd quickly buy something from nearby and return him his jacket. He told her there was no rush. She could return the jacket another time.

It was on this pretence they met again. Their second date was a lovely mixed bag of laughter, storytelling and competitive banter at Mr. Kericha's local pool club. And now they were ready for their third date. Janki had told Mr. Kericha how much she loved a stir-fry and so he had invited her to his place to sample her favourite dish cooked by him. He was due to get the table runner out, the wine glasses on the table and the plate warmer out to make an impression. He even put candles on the microwave so he would remember to light them and place them around the house for added ambiance.

What use was all his planning now that he was down a hole? What use was all that thought of ambiance now that he was down a hole? What would Janki think of him now? She overlooked him falling on their first meeting, she overlooked him bumping his head on a door in the second meeting but surely she wouldn't be able to overlook him falling down a hole on the day of what was meant to be their third meeting.

How would he explain it to her? How would he tell her the parrot died because he let her out of the cage, fell down a hole and then wasn't able to feed her in time? How would he tell her that he was going to change his top and he was going to change his socks to matching ones? How would he be able to make it to another date when it all looked so silly?

He had been shouting out for help for a while before help came his way. The neighbours, so occupied with their own lives, didn't even notice Mr. Kericha's pleas. It was Janki who heard that shout for help as she came to the front door. It seemed to be coming from the garden and so she went down to the garden through the side alleyway.

It was all so embarrassing having Janki see him like that but there wasn't much he could do. She was shocked to see Mr. Kericha down the hole but also a bit relieved. She was glad he was alive even if he looked a bit silly down in the hole. She was glad he had his consciousness and even his good humour.

She didn't care much for the odd socks or the ill-fitting top; she just wanted him out of the hole. She looked around and saw an old-looking jumper hanging on his washing line and decided to take it down. With his jumper, she tied a knot to her coat and threw it down to him. As he tried to pull himself out she realised her strength wouldn't be able to help him up. And so, after looking around and finding nothing to anchor it on, she felt miserable.

She was unable to help him and didn't know what to do. Mr. Kericha looked up at Janki and asked her to go indoors and pick up the keys for the shed. The keys were by the fridge, hanging on a nail. He said she wouldn't miss them. He also apologised and said the kitchen was a mess and he had hoped to have had it all cleared up by the time she came.

Later that day, Mr. Kericha sat with Janki laughing about the mess she saw in the kitchen, his ill-fitting clothes and Janki trying to open the shed door with that ever-so stiff lock. He thought back to his climbing out of that hole with the ladder Janki managed to lug out of the shed and to him but mostly he thought of how she had rushed to his rescue and had held his hand as he came out of the hole.

He remembered her cleaning up his kitchen and making a cup of tea for him whilst he was in the shower. When he came back to the room he was filled with joy. What a fantastic woman Janki was. In a day she had helped him out of a hole, given his kitchen a makeover and had made him a delightful and welcome cup of tea.

After all that it was only fair that he treated her to a lovely meal. The stir-fry was ready and just needed heating and as she sat on a stool by the table, he whipped up some rice. As the conversation flowed he forgot his timing on the rice. When he remembered it was too late, the rice was stuck to the pan and the grains to each other. There was no way Janki would be impressed now.

He wondered whether or not to serve the rice and when she asked what was keeping him, he told her. Janki laughed and said, 'That's OK, stir-fry with sticky rice! That's the best combination!'

Mr. Kericha looked at her and smiled. She somehow made all his clumsiness seem OK and it was for that reason he met her again and again. She met him again and again too. There was something about him that endeared her to him too. He was so different to everyone she had dated before. His funny bumbling ways made her smile and his humbleness and honesty felt genuine.

It had been years of dating unsuitable people that had made her join the dating agency. A part of her joined in desperation and a part of her joined to try her luck through an avenue she would never have considered years ago. All her dates over the last few years always seemed to follow the same pattern and nine times out of ten were just formulaic. She categorised the men she met into two camps; those that were more interested in themselves than her and those that pretended to be overly interested in her but clearly only had one thing on their dirty minds.

There was never any real balance. There was never any real variety and so no one ever really stood out. Mr.

Kericha was certainly not her 'usual' type and was certainly someone different. He fell into neither of the two camps and that felt refreshing and brand new. He was respectful, unassuming and sincere; all qualities Janki had been looking for in a partner. And so she met him again and again and again too.

Some of their dates were a right concoction of silliness and fun and some were more sombre and melancholic. There was a time when they both went to play mini golf and a group of young-looking guys tried to make passes at Janki in her beautiful teal coloured dress that snugly sat on her slender frame. The group of guys looked at Mr. Kericha and laughed at such an odd-looking pair.

'Tell your Dad that you want to play with us!' said one of the most confident and brazen in the group. Janki ignored the comments at first, as did Mr. Kericha.

'Come on Dad, let her play with us! Let her play with me!' said another one in the group licking his lips as he suggestively stroked his golf club.

'So immature!' Janki muttered under her breath as she looked at Mr. Kericha signaling to him to ignore their comments.

When they got to the 9th hole and the comments were still rolling in, Mr. Kericha turned to them and said, 'It's time you all go and ask *your* Dad's where your manners are!'

'OK granddad!' mocked one of them.

'Ask your granddad too! Let me and the most beautiful woman alive just play a game of golf...in peace! Yes she's stunning, but she's taken! So just zip it and leave her and me alone! If you don't, I'll call security and get you chucked out of here. Understood?'

'Just leave it Johnny,' said one of the guys to the most confident and brazen in the group. 'It's not worth it,' he said and then looking at Mr. Kericha and Janki he added, 'Carry on, he won't say anything.'

'Losers!' said Johnny before leaving Mr. Kericha and Janki to resume their game of golf in peace.

Janki looked at Mr. Kericha. In that whole silly incident, he had protected her, defended her and called her 'the most beautiful woman alive'. He had stood up to the group of idiots, peacefully diffused the situation and had called her stunning. Janki smiled, she had always wanted a man to be able to look out for her, shelter her from trouble and just be a hero. While she had been thinking of throwing golf balls at them, Mr. Kericha left the scene with his dignity intact.

Numerous dates followed where they had little situations that were silly but they were always so right too. Janki and Mr. Kericha enjoyed being there for one another and when Mr. Kericha proposed, he even dropped the engagement ring, which rolled down the hill he proposed to her on. Before Janki had a chance to give her answer, they both desperately ran to catch the ring before it fell into the duck pond that was nearby. With God's grace, the ring stopped centimetres from the pond and Janki and Mr. Kericha were beside themselves with joy at it being safe. They laughed as they looked at the ring. Going down on one knee, Mr. Kericha said,

'You keep the ring! I might drop it in the pond!' Laughing at the situation, Janki looked at her knight in shining armour as he dusted himself off before he continued, 'Janki, I didn't plan to do this next to this duck pond. I didn't plan for you to hold the ring while I did this. I didn't even plan to fall in love with you but I did, and I'm so glad. Janki, I love being in love with you. You're the one I want to spend the rest of my life with. You're the one I want to have babies with, build a home with, build a future with. I can't promise you everything will always be perfect but I can promise it will always be just right for us.' Looking at Janki's smile and her eyes glistening, he said, 'I want to marry you and be there for you always. Will you, Janki, be my wife? Will you marry me?'

'Yes,' she said as she hugged him. 'I'd love to marry you.' Placing the ring back in his hands, she added, 'Go on, put it on my finger.' Mr. Kericha put the ring on her finger and after embracing her and sharing a kiss, he jumped in the air and shouted, 'I love you, Janki Kericha! I love you, Mrs. Kericha!'

Years later, they found themselves laughing at the days before they got married and Sanju and Heena becoming their blessed children. They recalled Janki's button popping, her engagement ring nearly falling in the duck pond, Mr. Kericha falling down the hole and the sticky rice. It was all a bit laughable and all a bit silly but somehow it made them smile. It was all a bit laughable and all a bit silly but somehow it felt beautiful and just so very right.

ABOUT THE AUTHOR

TK Seehra has a M.A. in English Literature and has always had a keen interest in reading and writing English. She has been writing for years personally and professionally. Her poetry was selected to feature in an anthology, *Straight from the Heart* and she wrote for a literary magazine at the University of Westminster, *Raw Material*. She has contributed an article to *Target Medicine*, a medical journal and has written for printed and online publications in the NHS for staff and public audiences.

Follow her on Facebook and Twitter @tkseehra

Printed in Great Britain
by Amazon.co.uk, Ltd.,
Marston Gate.